The Canonical Epistle

Peter of Alexandria

Copyright Notice

The text in this book has been downloaded from the internet and has been extensively edited and typeset.

CONTENTS

CANON I	1
CANON II	5
CANON III	8
CANON IV	10
CANON V	13
CANON VI	18
CANON VII	20
CANON VIII	23
CANON IX	27
CANON X	34
CANON XI	47
CANON XII	54
CANON XIII	57
CANON XIV	62
CANON XV	66

I

THE CANONICAL EPISTLE, WITH THE COMMENTARIES OF THEODORE BALSA-MON AND JOHN ZONARAS.

THE CANONS OF THE BLESSED PETER, ARCHBISHOP OF ALEXANDRIA, AS THEY ARE GIVEN IN HIS SERMON ON PENI-TENCE.

CANON I

BUT since the fourth passover of the persecution has arrived, it is sufficient, in the case of those who have been apprehended and thrown into prison, and who have sustained torments not to be borne, and stripes intolerable, and many other dreadful afflictions, and afterwards have been betrayed by the frailty of the flesh, even though they were not at the first received On account of their grievous fall that followed yet because they contended sorely and resisted long; for they did not come to this of their own will, but were betrayed by the frailty of the flesh for they show in their bodies the marks of Jesus, and some are now, for the third year, bewailing their fault: it is sufficient, I say, that from the time of their submissive approach, other forty days should be enjoined upon them, to keep them in remembrance of these things; those forty days during which, though our Lord and Saviour Jesus Christ had fasted, He was yet, after He had been baptized, tempted of the devil. And when they shall have, during these days, exercised themselves much, and constantly fasted, then let them watch in prayer, meditating upon what was spoken by the Lord to him who tempted Him to fall down and worship him: "Get thee behind me, Satan; for it is written, Thou shall worship the Lord thy God, and Him only shalt thou serve. "

BALSAMON. The present canons treat of those who have in the persecution denied the faith, and are doing penance. And the first canon ordains, that upon those who after many torments have sacrificed to the gods, not being able by reason of frailty to persevere, and who have passed three years in penitence, other forty days should be enjoined, and that then they should be admitted into the Church. Observe these present canons which lay down various and useful rules in favour of those who have denied their God, and seek for repentance, anti concerning those who have of their own accord sought martyrdom, and have lapsed, and then have again confessed the faith, and other things of the like nature. Consult also, for you will profitably do so, many canons Of the Council of Ancyra.

ZONARAS. Amongst those who in these turbulent times denied the faith, the holy Peter makes a distinction, and says, that upon those who had been brought before the tyrant, and thrown into prison, and who had endured very grievous torments, and intolerable scourgings, and such as could be cured by no care or medicine (for anhkeston signifies medical care, and akos is the same as immedicabile), and other dreadful afflictions, and afterwards yielding, sacrificed to the gods, being betrayed as it were by the weakness of the flesh, which could not hold out under the pain unto the end, that for them the time past should suffice for punishment; since, indeed, says he, the fourth passover has now past since they made this very grievous fall. And although perhaps at first, when they approached in penitence, they, were not received, yet because they did not of their own freewill proceed to sacrifice to the gods, and resisted long, and hear about with them the marks of Jesus, that is to say, the scars of the wounds which, in behalf of Christ, they have endured, and the third year has now elapsed since they first bewailed their fall, he decrees that, as an additional punishment, other forty days from the time that they came asking to be admitted to communion should be enjoined on them in the place of any further severity; during which they should exercise a still greater degree of penance, and should fast more earnestly, that is, with more attentive care, keeping guard over themselves, being watchful in prayer, meditating upon, that is, turning over perpetually in their minds, and saying in words, the text quoted by the Lord against the tempter, "Get thee behind me, Satan; for it is written, Thou shalt worship the Lord thy God, and Him only shalt thou serve."

CANON II

But in the case of those who, after that they were thrown into prison, and in the dungeon, as in a place besieged, endured afflictions and nauseous odours, bill afterwards, without the conflict of torments, were led captive, being broken in spirit by poverty of strength, and a certain blindness of the understanding, a year in addition to the foregoing time will suffice; for they gave themselves up to be afflicted for the name of Christ, even though in their dungeon they enjoyed much consolation from their brethren; which, indeed, they shall return many fold, desiring to be set free from that most bitter captivity of the devil, especially remembering Him who said: "The spirit of the Lord is upon me, because He hath anointed me to preach the Gospel to the poor; He hath sent me to heal the brokenhearted, to preach deliverance to the captives, and recovering of sight to the blind, to set at liberty them that are bruised; to preach the acceptable year of the Lord, and the day of recompense unto our God. "

BALSAMON. This canon enacts that those who have only been evil entreated in prison, and who without torment have lapsed, should be punished after the three years with an additional year. For though they obtained consolation, certain of the faithful ministering to them the necessaries of life, yet they ought to obtain pardon, as being those who have suffered severely for the faith.

ZONARAS. In the second order, he places those who have only been thrown into prison, and evil entreated in the dungeon, and yet, though harassed by no torments, have offended; upon whom, besides the time past, the three years, namely, of which we have spoken, he proposes to inflict the penalty of an additional year, since they also, says he, have for Christ's name endured hardness, even though it may be that they obtained some consolation from the brethren whilst in prison. For it is probable that the faithful, who were not in custody, ministered to those in bonds the necessaries of life, and brought to them some alleviation of their lot. Which things, indeed, they shall return many fold; for those consolations which they enjoyed in prison they shall vex themselves with penance, and afflict themselves in diverse ways, if they wish to be set free from the captivity of the devil, having become his captives and slaves by their denial of Christ. He subjoins the word of the prophet, taken from Isaiah, which he says that they ought to keep in remembrance.

CANON III

But as for those who have suffered none of these things, and have shown no fruit of faith., but of their own accord have gone over to wickedness, being betrayed by fear and cowardice, and now come to repentance, it is necessary and convenient to propose the parable of the unfruitful fig-tree, as the Lord says: "A certain man had a fig-tree planted in his vineyard; and he came and sought fruit thereon, and found none. Then said he unto the dresser of his vineyard, Behold, these three years I come seeking fruit on this fig-tree, and find none: cut it down; why cumbereth it the ground? And he answering, said unto him, Lord, let it alone this year also, till I shall dig about it, and dung it. And if it bear fruit, well; and if not, then alter mat thou shall cut it down." Keeping this before their eyes, and showing forth fruit worthy of repentance, after so long an interval of time, they will be profiled.

BALSAMON. Those who from fear only and timidity deserted the faith, and then had an eye towards repentance, the canon punishes with three years' exclusion, according to the parable of the fig-tree in the Gospels. For the Lord said, Three years I come to it seeking fruit, and find none; but the vinedresser replies, Lord, let it alone this year also.

ZONARAS. But those, he says, who having suffered no hardness, have deserted from fear only and timidity, in that they of their own accord have approached to wickedness; and then looked towards repentance, their case the parable of the fig-tree in the Gospels will exactly suit. Let them keep this before their eyes, and show forth for an equal period labours worthy of penitence, and they shall be profited; that is, after the fourth year. For the Lord said, Three years I come to it seeking fruit, and find none; and the vinedresser answered, Lord, let it alone this year also.

CANON IV

To those who are altogether reprobate, and unrepentant, who possess the Ethiopian's unchanging skin, and the leopard's spots, it shall be said, as it was spoken to another fig-tree, "Let no fruit grow on thee henceforward for ever; and it presently withered away. " For in them is fulfilled what was spoken by the Preacher: "That which is crooked cannot be made straight; and that which is wanting cannot be numbered. " For unless that which is crooked shall first he made straight, it is impossible for it to be adorned; and unless that which is wanting shall first be made up, it cannot be numbered. Hence also, in the end, will happen unto them what is spoken by Esaias the prophet: "They shall look upon the carcases of the men that have transgressed against Me; for their worm shall not die, neither shall their fire be quenched; and they shall be an abhorring unto all flesh. " Since as by the same also has been predicted, "But the wicked are like the troubled sea, when it cannot rest, whose waters cast up mire and dirt. There is no peace, saith my God, to the wicked. "

BALSAMON. What has been previously said of the lapsed, has been said of the repentant. But against those who are unrepentant, he brings forward the cursing of another fig-tree, to which the Lord said, because of its unprofitableness, "No fruit grow on thee henceforward for ever."

ZONARAS. What has been previously said of the lapsed, has been said of the repentant. Against those whom, from desperation or depraved opinion, are impenitent, and carry about with them perpetually the inherent and indelible blackness of sin, as of an Ethiopian's skin, or the leopard's spots, he brings forward the cursing of another fig-tree. To which the Lord said for its barrenness, "Let no fruit grow on thee henceforward for ever. And he says that in them must be fulfilled that word of the Preacher: "That which is crooked cannot be made straight; and that which is wanting cannot be numbered." Then having explained these things, he subjoins the words of Isaiah.

CANON V

But upon those who have used dissimulation like David, who reigned himself to be mad to avoid death, being not mad in reality; and those who have not nakedly written down their denial of the faith, but being in much tribulation, as boys endowed with sagacity and prudence amongst foolish children, have mocked the snares of their enemies, either passing by the altars, or giving a writing, or sending heathen to do sacrifice instead of themselves, even though some of them who have confessed have, as I have heard, pardoned individuals of them, since with the greatest caution they have avoided to touch the fire with their own hands, and to offer incense to the impure demons; yet inasmuch as they escaped the notice of their persecutors by doing this, let a penalty of six months' penance be imposed upon them. For thus will they be the rather profited, meditating upon the prophet's words, and saying, "Unto us a child is born, unto us a Son is given; and the government shall be upon His shoulder: and His name shall be called the Messenger of My mighty counsel." Who, as ye know, when another infant in the sixth month of his conception had preached before His coming repentance for the remission of sins, was himself also conceived to preach repentance. Moreover, we hear both also preaching, in the first place, not only repentance, but the kingdom of heaven, which, as we have learned, is within us; for the word which we believe is near us, in our mouth, and in our heart; which they, being put in remembrance of, will learn to confess with their mouths that Jesus is the Christ; believing in their heart that God hath raised him from the dead, and being as those who hear, that "with the heart man believeth unto righteousness; and with the mouth confession is made unto salvation."

BALSAMON. But if any have pretended to approach the altars, or to write their denial of the faith, and have not done this nakedly and openly, but by reigned arts have illuded those who offered them violence, as David did, who, when he was flying from Saul, and was amongst strangers, feigned himself to be mad, and thus escaped death. So they mocked the snares of their enemies, as children endowed with wisdom and prudence mock foolish children; for they deceived the impious heathen, in that they seemed to sacrifice, although they did not sacrifice, or perhaps they suborned heathens and infidels to take their place, and by these means they thought that they offered sacrifice; for them, he says, a period of six months will suffice for penance. For although they did not sacrifice, yet because they promised to sacrifice, or sent others to do so in their place, they are thought to stand in need of repentance, even though some of those who have given their testimony for the faith have pardoned individuals of them. He compares them to children, as not having manfully withstood the idolaters, but to prudent children, because by artifice they avoided doing sacrifice.

ZONARAS. But if any have pretended to approach the altars, or to write their denial of the faith, but have not nakedly written down their abnegation, that is, not manifestly, not openly; but by a sort of trick have cheated those who offered them violence; as David, who while lie was flying from Saul, and bad come amongst strange people, reigned himself to be mad, and in this way avoided death. They mocked indeed, he children, endowed with wisdom and sagacity, and those says, the insidious devices of their enemies; as prudent who skilfully take counsel, deceive foolish children. Now be compares those to prudent children by whom the impious heathen were deceived, and those who though they did not sacrifice, yet seemed to sacrifice, prudent indeed, as having thus far avoided sacrificing; but children, in that they did not show forth a mature and manly spirit, and did not nobly resist the worshippers of idols, but covenanted to sacrifice, even though they suborned some in their places, heathens, forsooth, and infidels, and when these sacrificed, they were considered to have sacrificed. For men of this sort, he says, a period of six months will suffice for penance. For although they did not sacrifice, yet because they covenanted to sacrifice, or suborned others to do so, and thus themselves appeared to have sacrificed, they were judged to stand in need of repentance; even though some confessors might have pardoned individuals of them; for some of those who witnessed to the faith and suffered for it, pardoned those who by an artifice, as has been said, escaped offering sacrifice, and admitted them to communion with the faithful, because they studiously avoided offering sacrifice to demons. And on account of the fixing of this term of six months, he calls to remembrance the annunciation made by Gabriel, in the sixth month of the conception of the Forerunner, in which the Lord was conceived. Then he subjoins the words of the apostle.

CANON VI

In the case of those who have sent Christian slaves to offer sacrifice for them, the slaves indeed as being in their master's hands, and in a manner themselves also in the custody of their masters, and being threatened by them, and from their fear having come to this pass and having lapsed, shall during the year show forth the works of penitence, learning for the future, as the slaves of Christ, to do the will of Christ and to fear Him, listening to this especially, that "whatsoever good thing any man doeth, the same shall he receive of the Lord, whether he be bond or free."

BALSAMON. The slaves who under the commands and threatenings of their masters offered sacrifice, this father punishes with a year's exclusion; yet he pardons them as having acted under the orders of a master, and does not inflict a heavy punishment upon them. But yet since they are much more the servants of Christ, even as they ought to fear

Him more, he imposes on them a moderate punishment; for, as says the great Paul, "whatsoever good thing any man doeth, the same shall he receive of the Lord, whether he be bond or free."

ZONARAS. Some have sent their own Christian servants, even against their will, to offer sacrifice in their stead. These servants, therefore, although not of their own freewill, but being compelled by their masters, they offered sacrifice, this father ordains shall pass a year in penance, and enjoins them to remember that, being of the number of the faithful, they are the servants of Christ, and that Him they ought rather to fear; for "whatsoever any man doeth," says the great apostle, "the same shall he receive, whether he be bond or free."

CANON VII

But the freemen shall be tried by penance for three years, both for their dissimulation, and for having compelled their fellow-servants to offer sacrifice, inasmuch as they have not obeyed the apostle, who would have the masters do the same things unto the servant, forbearing threatening; knowing, says he, that our and their Master is in heaven; and that there is no respect of persons with Him. Now, if we all have one Master, with whom is no respect of persons, since Christ is all and in all, in barbarian, Scythian, bond or free, they ought to consider what they have done, wishing to preserve their own lives. They have drawn their fellow-servants to idolatry who would have been able to escape, had they given to them that which is just and equal, as again says the apostle.

BALSAMON. But upon the freemen, or the masters of the servant compelled to sacrifice, he enjoins a punishment of three years, both because they pretended to sacrifice, and seemed to assent to it; and also because they compelled their fellow-servants to offer sacrifice, and did not obey the apostle, who ordered them to forbear threatening their servants, inasmuch as they themselves, the masters, are the servants of God, and fellow-servants with their own domestics And then they have made haste to preserve their own lives, and have driven their fellow-servants to idolatry who might have escaped.

ZONARAS. But upon the freemen, that is, the masters of the servants who were compelled to sacrifice, he enjoins a penalty of three years, both because they pretended to sacrifice, and altogether appeared to succumb; and also because they compelled their fellow-servants to offer sacrifice, and did not obey the apostle's injunction to forbear threatening their servants; since they also, the masters, are the servants of God, and the fellow-servants of their own domestics. And they indeed made haste to preserve their own lives, and drove their fellow-servants, who might have escaped, to idolatry.

CANON VIII

But to those who have been delivered up, and have fallen, who also of their own accord have approached the contest, confessing themselves to be Christians, and have been tormented and thrown into prison, it is right with joy and exultation of heart to add strength, and to communicate to them in all things, both in prayer, and in partaking of the body and blood of Christ, and in hortatory discourse; in order that contending the more constantly, they may be counted worthy of "the prize of their high calling." For "seven times," he says, "a just man falleth, and riseth up again," which, indeed, if all that have lapsed had done, they would have shown forth a most perfect penitence, and one which penetrates the whole heart.

BALSAMON. Some had had information laid against them before the tyrant, and had been delivered up, or themselves had of their own accord given themselves up, and then being overcome by their torments, had failed in their testimony. Afterwards repenting, and acknowledging what was right and good, they confessed themselves to he Christians, so that they were cast into prison, and afflicted with torments. These this holy man thinks it right to receive with joy of heart, and to confirm in the orthodox faith, and to communicate with, both in prayers and in partaking of the sacraments, and to exhort with cheering words, that they may be more constant in the contest, and counted worthy of the heavenly kingdom. And that it might not be thought that they ought not to be received, because they hart lapsed, he brings forward the testimony of Scripture to the effect that "seven times," that is, often, "the just man falleth, and riseth up again." And, says he, if all who have failed in their confession had done this, namely, taken up their struggle again, and before the tyrant confessed themselves to be Christians, they would have shown forth a most perfect penitence. The subject, therefore, comprehended in this canon differs from that contained in the first canon, for there indeed those who by reason of their torment had lapsed, were not converted so as to confess the faith before the tyrants; but here those who by reason of their torment have lapsed, with a worthy penitence, confess the Lord before the tyrants, wherefore they are reckoned not to have fallen.

ZONARAS. But, says he, if any have had information laid against them before the tyrants, and have been delivered up, or have of themselves given themselves up, and being overcome by the violence of their torments have failed in their testimony, not being able to endure the distresses and afflictions with which in the dungeon they were afflicted; and afterwards taking up the contest anew, have confessed themselves to be Christians, so that they have been again cast into prison and afflicted with torments: such men this holy martyr judges it reasonable that they should be joyfully received; and that they should be strengthened, that is, have strength, spirit, and confidence added to them, in order that they may confess the faith, and that they should be communi-cared with in all things, both in prayer, and in partaking of the sacraments, and that they should be exhorted with loving words, to rouse themselves to give testimony to the faith, that they may be more constant in the contest, and counted worthy of the heavenly kingdom. And that it might not he thought by any that they ought not to be received from the fact that they had lapsed, and sacrificed to the idols, he brings forth this testimony from Holy Scripture: "Seven times," that is, often, "the just man falleth, and riseth up again." And, says be, if all who have failed in their confession had done this, that is, after their fall, taken up the contest afresh, and confessed themselves to be Christians before the tyrants, they would have given proof of a most perfect repentance.

CANON IX

With those also who, as it were from sleep, themselves leap forth upon a contest which is travailing long and likely to be protracted, and draw upon themselves the temptations as it were of a sea-fight, and the inundations of many waves, or rather are for the brethren kindling the coals of the sinners, with them also we must communicate, inasmuch as they come to this in the name of Christ, even though they take no heed unto His words, when He teaches us "to pray that we enter not into temptation;" and again in His prayer, He says to His Father, "and lead us not into temptation, but deliver us from evil." And perhaps also they know not that the Master of the House and our Great Teacher often retired from those who would lay snares for Him, and that sometimes He walked not openly because of them; and even when the time of His passion drew on, He delivered not up Himself, but waited until they came to Him with "swords and staves." He said to them therefore, "Are ye come out, as against a thief with swords and staves, for to take Me?" And they "delivered Him," He says, "to Pilate." As it was with Him it happens to those who walk keeping Him before them as an example, recollecting His divine words, in which, confirming us, He speaks of persecution: "Take heed unto yourselves, for they will deliver you up to the councils, and they will scourge you in their synagogues." Now, He says, they will deliver you up, and not, ye shall deliver up yourselves; and "ye shall be brought before rulers and kings for My sake," but not, ye shall bring yourselves, for He would have us pass from place to place as long as there are those who persecute us for His name's sake; even as again we hear Him saying, "But when they persecute you in this city, flee ye into another." For He would not have us go over to the ministers and satellites of the devil, that we might not be the cause to them of a manifold death, inasmuch as thus we should be compelling them both to be harsher, and to carry out their deadly works, but He would have us to wait, and to take heed to ourselves, to watch and to pray, lest we enter into temptation. Thus first Stephen, pressing on His footsteps, suffered martyrdom, being apprehended in Jerusalem by the transgressors, and being brought before the council, he was stoned, and glorified for the name of Christ, praying with the words, "Lord, lay not this sin to their charge." Thus James, in the second place, being of Herod apprehended, was beheaded with the sword. Thus Peter, the first of the apostles, having been often apprehended, and thrown into prison, and treated with igominy, was last of all crucified at Rome. Likewise also, the renowned Paul having been oftentimes delivered up and brought in peril of death, having endured many evils, and making his boast in his numerous persecutions and afflictions, in the same city was also himself beheaded; who, in the things in which he gloried, in these also ended his life; and at Damascus he was let down by night in a basket by the wall, and escaped the hands of him who sought to take him. For what they set before themselves, first and foremost, was to do the work of an evangelist, and to teach the Word of God, in which, confirming the brethren, that they might continue in the faith, they said this also, "that we must out of much tribulation enter into the kingdom of God." For they sought not what was profitable for them, but that which was profitable for the many, that they might be saved, and that they might be enabled to say unto them many things conducing to this, that they might act suitably to the Word of God, "unless," as says the apostle, "the time should fail me in speaking."

BALSAMON. Those who have but just arisen from sleep, and especially if they were weighed down with a heavy and profound sleep, have no constant reason, hut one perturbed and unsteady. To such as these this blessed martyr likens those who, not in due order, but rashly and inconsiderately, thrust themselves upon the contest, which is as it were in travail, and delayed and protracted, inasmuch as it has not vet burst forth openly, but meditates and delays, hesitating in truth to bring forth the combatants, who bring temptation upon themselves, or draw it towards them. Now these especially are, for the rest of the faithful, kindling the coals of the sinners, that is to say, the punishment of the tyrants. But although he reprehends those who act so, yet he enjoins the faithful nevertheless to communicate with them, because on account of Christ they have undergone the contest, even though they have ignored His teaching, for He teaches them to pray that they may not be tempted; and He did not deliver up Himself, but was delivered up; and we are not to go over to the tormentors, that we may not be the cause of bringing upon them the guilt of many murders, as those do who incite them to inflict punishment upon the godly. The canon brings forward different examples from Holy Scripture.

ZONARAS. Those who have recently arisen from sleep, especially if they were oppressed with a heavy sleep, have no steady reason, but one inconstant and perturbed. To men of this sort this holy martyr likens those who rush upon the contest, that is, those who, not in due course, but rashly and inconsiderately, intrude themselves upon it. It is, as it were, in travail, and delayed and protracted, inasmuch as it has not yet burst forth openly, but meditates and delays, and hesitates to bring forth the combatants, who bring temptation upon themselves, that is, draw it towards themselves, or rather, for the rest of the faithful, kindle the coals of the sinners, the torments, namely, which are by the tyrants inflicted. But although he finds fault with those who act in this way, he nevertheless decrees that the faithful must communicate with them, because in the name of Christ they come forward to this, trusting, that is, in Christ, or in His name demanding this trial for themselves, even though, perhaps, they are not obeying His precepts; for He taught them to pray that they might not be tempted; and they are ignoring the fact too that the Lord retired from those who were laying snares for Him, and was wont sometimes to walk not openly; neither did He give up Himself to His passion, but was given up by others; and He commanded His disciples, when their enemies persecuted them, to fly from city to city, and not of their own accord to give themselves up to the tormentors, lest they should be the cause of bringing the guilt of much blood upon their heads, irritating them as it were to inflict punishment upon godly men. And he brings forward the example of the apostles, of Stephen, of James, and the chiefs of the order, Peter and Paul.

CANON X

Whence it is not right either that those of the clergy who have deserted of their own accord, and have lapsed, and taken up the contest afresh, should remain any longer in their sacred office, inasmuch as they have left destitute the flock of the Lord, and brought blame upon themselves, which thing did not one of the apostles. For when the blessed apostle Paul had undergone many persecutions, and had shown forth the prizes of many contests, though he knew that it was far better to "depart, and to be with Christ," yet he brings this forward, and says, "Nevertheless to abide in the flesh is more needful for you." For considering not his own advantage but the advantage of many, that they might be saved, he judged it more necessary than his own rest to remain with the brethren, and to have a care for them; who also would have him that teacheth to be "in doctrine" an example to the faithful. Whence it follows that those who, contending in prison, have fallen from their ministry, and have again taken up the struggle, are plainly wanting in perception. For how else is it that they seek for that which they have left, when in this present time they can be useful to the brethren? For as long as they remained firm and stable, of that which they had done contrary to reason, of this indulgence was accorded them. But when they lapsed, as having carried themselves with ostentation, and brought reproach upon themselves, they can no longer discharge their sacred ministry; and, therefore, let them the rather take heed to pass their life in humility, ceasing from vainglory. For communion is sufficient for them, which is granted them with diligence and care for two causes; both that they should not seem to be afflicted with sorrow, and hence by violence seize on their departure from this world; and also lest any of the lapsed should have a pretext for being remiss by occasion of the punishment. And these indeed will reap more shame and ignominy than all others, even as he who laid the foundation and was not able to finish it; for "all that pass by," He says, "will begin to mock him, saying, "This man laid the foundation, and was not able to finish it.""

BALSAMON. The father having spoken of those who of their own accord went over to the contest of martyrdom, now also speaks of those of the clergy who are in such a case, and he says, that if any clergyman hath of his own accord sought the contest, and then, not being able to bear the tortures, has fallen, but returning to himself, has recanted his error, and before the tyrants confessed himself a Christian, such a one shall no longer discharge his sacred ministry, because he hath deserted the Lord's flock, and because, having of his own accord sought the contest, through not being able to endure the torment, he hath brought reproach upon himself. For to neglect the teaching of the people, and to prefer their own advantage, this did not the apostles. For the mighty Paul, after that he had endured many torments, though he perceived that it was far better to leave this life, yet chose rather to live and to be tormented for the salvation and instruction of the people. They are therefore altogether devoid of perception who seek the sacred ministry from which they have fallen of their own accord. For how is it that they seek for that which they have left, when they are able in this season of persecution, that is, to be useful to their brethren? If indeed they had not fallen, of that which they had done contrary to reason, their spontaneous flight for instance, or their slackness in teaching and confirming the brethren, of these things indulgence would be extended to them. But if from their own arrogance and conceit they have lapsed, – for of such a nature is it rashly to venture to expose themselves to torture, and not to be able to endure it, and thus a triumph has been gained over them, – they cannot any longer execute their sacred office. Wherefore let them the rather take heed that they perfect their confession by humility, ceasing from the vainglory of seeking for the sacred ministry; for communion with the faithful is sufficient for them, which is granted for two reasons, with diligent caution, and just judgment. For if we say that we will not hold them to be communicants, we shall both afflict them with grief, giving our sentence as it were that they should depart this life with violence; and we shall cause others also, who may have lapsed, and wish to return to what is right, to be negligent and remiss in this respect, having as a pretext, that they will not be admitted to communicate with the faithful, even though after their fall they should confess the faith, who, if they are not converted, will undergo more shame and ignominy than others, even as he who laid the foundation, and did not finish the building. For such a one do those resemble, who, for Christ's sake indeed, have offered themselves to be tormented, and having laid as it were a good foundation, have not been able to perfect that which is good by reason of their fall. Observe, then, that not even confession for Christ's sake restores him who has once lapsed and thus become an alien from his clerical office.

ZONARAS. The father having spoken of those who have of their own accord exposed themselves to the contest of martyrdom, now begins to discourse about those of the clergy who have done the same thing; and says that if any clergyman has of his own accord given himself up, and then, not being able to endure the violence of the torment, has fallen, and again recollecting himself has roused himself afresh to the contest, and has confessed himself a Christian before the tyrants, a man of this sort is not any longer to be admitted to the sacred ministry. And the reason of this he subjoins; because he has forsaken the Lord's flock, and because having of his own accord offered himself to the enemy, and not having with constancy endured his torments, he has brought reproach upon himself. But that they should despise the instruction of the people, and prefer their own advantage, this did not the apostles. For the mighty Paul, though he had endured many torments, and felt that it was better for him to leave this life, preferred to live and to be tormented for the salvation and instruction of the people. Wherefore he demonstrates those to be altogether devoid of perception who ask for the sacred ministry from which they have voluntarily fallen. For how is it, says he, that they ask for that which they have left, when in a season of this sort, of raging persecution forsooth, they can be of great assistance to the brethren? As long as they were free from the charge of having lapsed, they would have obtained pardon for their action that was rashly undertaken, that, namely, of voluntarily offering themselves to the adversary, or their negligence in instructing the brethren. But since they have fallen, inasmuch as they have acted ostentatiously, they are not to be permitted any longer to discharge their sacred functions. If, says he, that they had not fallen they would have obtained pardon for their action which was devoid of reason; calling that action devoid of reason, not only because they gave themselves up to the enemy, but rather because they deserted the Lord's flock, and did not remain to guard it, and to confirm the brethren who were harassed in this time of persecution. But if they have fallen, from the fact that they have carried themselves vauntingly, and he here calls pride and arrogance perpereia , because it is from arrogance that they have put confidence in themselves, and have put an end to the contest, and have brought reproach upon themselves; that is, by reason of their fall, they have contracted a blemish and stain, it is not lawful for them any longer to be occupied in the sacred ministry. Wherefore let them study, says he, to perfect their confession by humility, ceasing forsooth from all vainglory. For in that they seek to be enrolled in the sacred ministry, this proceeds from ambition and self-seeking. For communion is sufficient for them, that the faithful should communicate with them, and pray with them, and that they should participate in the sacred mysteries. And this should be granted with diligent caution and care, both lest they should seem to be afflicted with grief, seizing on a dissolution of this life, lest, that is, as he says, being overcome with grief, they should depart and get free from the body, that is, go out from it, from the violence of the torment and afflictions which they undergo in the prison; and that none should have the pretext of their punishment for carrying themselves dissolutely and cowardly in the contest of confession, and thus fall away. Who will the rather be put to shame, according to the saying in the Gospel, "Who could not finish after that he had laid the foundation."

Moreover, let those apply their minds to what is in this place brought forward by this great father and holy martyr, who say that it is lawful for bishops to give up their Sees, and to retain the dignity of the priesthood. For if to the clergy who voluntarily offered themselves to the contest of confession, and who, when tormented, failed in constancy and yielded, and afterwards returned to the contest, if to them indulgence is scarcely granted, because they deferred to execute their ministerial duties; nor, in the opinion of this divine father, is any thing else objected to them but that they deserted the brethren, when in adverse and turbulent times they might have been useful in confirming them in the faith, and that after that they had been counted worthy to bear testimony to the faith, and carried about in their flesh shall that chief priest and the marks of Christ; how pastor, who ought to lay down his life for the sheep, when he has deserted the flock that was committed unto him, and repudiated its care and administration, and as far as in him lies given it over to the wolf, be thought worthy to retain the dignity of the sacred ministry, and not rather be judged worthy of the severest punish-meats for deserting the people entrusted to his care? Nay, but he will demand a reward for this thing, or rather he will himself supply it to himself: refusing that which brings labour to them, namely, the office of teaching and of correcting vice; but embracing that which gains for them honour and glory, making it their own, keeping hold of it with their teeth as it were, and not letting it go in the least. For if in the case of the clergy it be called an action contrary to reason to desert the people, and to go away from them to the contest in the cause of piety; how much more contrary to reason shall it be judged for a bishop to desert his people, not in order that he may contend in a contest, but that he may deliver himself up to ease and indolence, and lay aside and escape entirely from his cares for the salvation of souls? The sixteenth canon also of the Seventh OEcumenical Council gravely accuses those of folly who decree that the dignity of the sacred ministry can be retained by a bishop who has repudiated his bishopric. For if according to the sentence of the aforesaid canon, a bishop who has been absent from his See more than six months, unless some one of the causes there enumerated shall have intervened, has both fallen from the episcopate and the highest dignity of the priesthood, and is deprived of both; how shall he who has repudiated the episcopate, and refuses any longer to feed the flock entrusted to him, and despises the care of it through his desire of an easy life, be held to be of the number of bishops? For if he who has committed the lesser fault, of leaving for more than six months the people placed under him destitute of the care and administration of a pastor, incurs the privation of the episcopate and of his sacred dignity; he who offends in a way greater and much more grievous, namely, in deserting altogether the multitude which the grace of the Holy Spirit has committed to him to be cared for and guarded, shall deservedly be punished with greater severity, and will pay the heavier penalty of losing, as far as he is concerned, the flock of which he was appointed shepherd by the great and chief Shepherd and High Priest. But those who decree the dignity of the priesthood to him as a reward and honorarium for declining his office, in my opinion make both themselves and him obnoxious to the judgment of God.

CANON XI

For those who first, when the persecution waxed warm, leaped forth, standing around the judgment-seat, and beholding the holy martyrs who were hastening to the "prize of their high calling," then, fired with a holy zeal, gave themselves up to this, using much boldness, and especially when they saw those who were drawn aside and lapsed, on their account they were roused mightily within, and, as it were by some inward voice, impelled to war down and subdue the adversary who was exulting; for this they earnestly contended, that he might not seem "to be wise in his own conceit," on account of those things in which by reason of his subtlety they appeared to be inferior to him, even though it escaped his observation that he was overcome by those who with constancy endured the torments of the lash and scourge, and the sharp edge of the sword, the burning in the fire, and the immersion in the water. To those also who entreat that the prayers and supplications of faith should be made either in behalf of those who have been punished by imprisonment, and have been delivered up by hunger and thirst, or for those who out of prison have by the judges been tortured with whippings and scourgings, and afterwards have been overcome by the infirmity of the flesh, it is right to give our consent. For to sympathize with the sorrow and affliction of those who sorrow and mourn for those who in the contest have been overcome by the great strength of the evil-contriving devil, whether it be for parents, or brethren, or children, hurts no one. For we know that on account of the faith of others some have obtained the goodness of God, both in the remission of sins, and in the health of their bodies, and in the resurrection of the dead. Therefore, being mindful of the many labours and distresses which for the name of Christ they have sustained, since they have themselves also repented, and have bewailed that which was done by them through their being betrayed by the languor and mortification of the body; and since, besides this, they testify that in their life they have as it were been aliens from their city, let us pray together with them and entreat for their reconciliation, together with other things that are befitting, through Hint who is "our Advocate with the Father, and makes propitiation for our sins." "And if any man sin," says he, "we have an Advocate with the Father, Jesus Christ the righteous: and He is the propitiation for our sins."

BALSAMON. The saint having said before that those who of their own accord entered upon the contest and lapsed, and did not repent nor recant their error, would be covered with more shame, as being like men who did not go on with the building beyond the foundation, that is, did not perfect that which is good, now brings forward a confirmation of this and other matters, saying, Those who taking their stand in the fervour and vehemence of the persecution, seeing the holy martyrs, and with what divine zeal they contended to receive the celestial crown, gave themselves up to martyrdom with much boldness, and especially when they saw some drawn aside, that is, led astray and deluded by the devil, and lapsing or denying godliness; wherefore being inwardly inflamed, and with hearts enkindled, as hearing that they by this means should war down and subdue the proud adversary the devil, were eager to undergo martyrdom lest the the devil should boast and seem "to be wise in his own conceit," as having by his subtlety and malice overcome those who of their own accord sought martyrdom: even though it escaped him that he was rather overcome by those combatants who bravely withstood the torments. Therefore to the faithful who pary for those who are enduring punishment, and afflicted by it is right to assent or to concur in this, which is also decreed; and it can by no means be hurtful to sympathize in their sorrow and affliction with the parents or other relatives in behalf of those who have given their testimony and undergone martyrdom, but have lapsed by the arts and snares of the devil. For we know that many have obtained the goodness and compassion of God by the prayers of others. Therefore we will pray for them that remission of their sins be granted them by God; and with the others who have lapsed, and have afterwards recanted their error, and confessed godliness, we will communicate, being mindful of those contests which before their fall they sustained for God's sake, and also of their subsequent worthy repentance, and that they testify that on account of their sin they have been as it were aliens from their city; and we will not only communicate with them, but pray also for their reconciliation, together with other things that are convenient, either with the good works which ought to be done by them – fasting, for instance, almsgiving, and penance; by which things He who is our Advocate makes the Father propitious towards us. Then he makes use of a passage of Holy Scripture, and this is taken from the first catholic epistle of the holy apostle and evangelist John.

ZONARAS. The meaning of the present canon is as follows:– Those, he says, who set in the fervour of the persecution, that is, in its greatest height and most vehement heat, beheld the martyrdoms of the saints, and how eagerly they hastened to receive the celestial crown, fired with a holy emulation, gave themselves up to martyrdom, leaping as it were into the contest with much boldness, in imitation of the saints who suffered, and offered themselves readily for the confirming of the faith by their testimony; and on that account especially, because they behold many who were drawn aside, that is, led astray, denying their faith. Whereupon they being inflamed, that is, tired in heart, endeavoured to subdue the adversary that was hostile to them, that he might not, as a victor, exult over the godly. Although it escaped him that he was rather conquered by them, many even unto death showing forth constancy for the faith. They hastened, therefore, says he, to do this, but overcome by the violence of their torments, by reason of the infirmity of the flesh, being some of them evil entreated in prison, and others punished by decree of the judges, and not being able to endure their punishment. It is meet, therefore, to sympathize with those who mourn for their sakes. Now they mourn, says he, some the lapse of parents, others of brethren, and others of children. To mourn, therefore, with those who bewail the lapsed, hurts no one; neither to join in prayer and grief with those who pray for themselves, together with other things that are reasonable, namely, that they who have lapsed may show forth other things that are consistent with penitence; such as are fasting and tears and other humiliations, and observe the punishment inflicted on them, and, if their means allow, bestow money upon the poor; by which means He who is the Advocate in our behalf will render the Father propitious to us. Then he brings forward a passage from Holy Scripture, which is taken from the first epistle of the holy apostle and evangelist John.

CANON XII

Against those who have given money that they might be entirely undisturbed by evil, an accusation cannot be brought. For they have sustained the loss and sacrifice of their goods that they might not hurt or destroy their soul, which others for the sake of filthy lucre have not done; and yet the Lord says, "What is a man profited, if he shall gain the whole world, and lose his own soul?" and again, "Ye cannot serve God and mammon." In these things, then, they have shown themselves the servants of God, inasmuch as they have hated, trodden under foot, and despised money, and have thus fulfilled what is written: "The ransom of a man's life are his riches." For we read also in the Acts of the Apostles that those who in the stead of Paul and Silas were dragged before the magistrates at Thessalonica, were dismissed with a heavy fine. For after that they had been very burdensome to them for his name, and had troubled the people and the rulers of the city, "having taken security," he says, "of Jason, and of the others, they let them go. And the brethren immediately sent away Paul and Silas by night unto Berea."

BALSAMON. After that the saint had finished his discourse concerning those who of their own accord had offered themselves to martyrdom, he said that those were not to be reprehended who by a sum of money paid down freed themselves from the affliction of persecution. For they preferred to make a sacrifice of their money rather than of their souls. Then he confirms this, and brings forward different Scripture examples from the Acts of the Apostles concerning the blessed apostle Paul and others.

ZONARAS. But those, he says, are not to be reprehended who have paid money down, and thus escaped, and maintained their piety, nor for this thing may any one bring an accusation against them. For they have preferred to lose their money rather than their souls, and have shown that they wish to serve God and not mammon; that is, riches. And he brings forward the words of Scripture, and the example, as in the Acts of the Apostles, of the blessed apostle Paul and others. Now, when it is said that they have been undisturbed by all evil? it is to be so taken, either that they have been left undisturbed, so far as the denial of the faith is concerned, which overcomes all evil, or he means the afflictions of persecutions.

CANON XIII

Hence neither is it lawful to accuse those who have left all, and have retired for the safety of their life, as if Others had been held back by them. For at Ephesus also they seized Gaius and Aristarchus instead of Paul, and rustled to the theatre, these being Paul's companions in travel and he wishing himself to enter in unto the people, since it was by reason of his having persuaded them, and drawing away a great multitude to the worship of the true God, that the tumult arose. "The disciples suffered him not," he says. "Nay, moreover, certain of the chief of Asia, who were his friends, sent unto him, desiring him that he would not adventure himself into the theatre." But if any persist in contending with them, let them apply their minds with sincerity to him who says, "Escape for thy life; look not behind thee." Let them recall to their minds also how Peter, the chief of the apostles, "was thrown into prison, and delivered to four quaternions of soldiers to keep him;" of whom, when he had escaped by night, and had been preserved out of the hand of the Jews by the commandment of the angel of the Lord, it is said, "As soon as it was day, there was no small stir among the soldiers, what was become of Peter. And when Herod had sought for him, and found him not, he examined the keepers, and commanded that they should be put to death," on account of whom no blame is attributed to Peter; for it was in their power, when they saw what was done, to escape, just as also all the infants in Bethlehem, and all the coast thereof, might have escaped, if their parents had known what was going to happen. These were put to death by the murderer Herod, in order to secure the death of one Infant whom he sought, which Infant itself also escaped at the commandment of the angel of the Lord, who now began quickly to spoil, and to hasten the prey, according to the name whereby he was called: as it is written, "Call his name Maher-shalal-hash-baz: for before the child shall have knowl-edge to cry, My father and my mother, the riches of Damascus anti the spoil of Samaria shall be taken away before the king of Assyria." The Magi then as now having been despoiled and divided for a prey, humbly, and in the guise of suppliants, adore the Child, opening their treasurers, and offering unto Him gifts most opportune and magnificent – gold, and frankincense, and myrrh – as to a king, to God, and to man; whence they were no longer willing to return to the Assyrian king, being forbidden to do so by Providence. For "being warned of God in a dream," he says, "that they should not return to Herod, they depart-ed into their own country another way." Hence the bloodthirsty "Herod, when he saw that he was mocked of the wise men, was exceeding wroth, and sent forth," he says, "and slew all the chil-dren that were in Bethlehem, and in all the coast thereof, from two years old and under, according to the time that he had diligently inquired of the wise men." Together with whom, having sought to kill another infant that had been previously born, and not being able to find him, he slew the child's father Zacharias between the temple and the altar, the child having escaped with his mother Elisabeth. Whence these men that have withdrawn themselves are not at all to be blamed.

BALSAMON. But if any, says he, have left their good and gone away, lest they should be detailed and brought into peril, as being those perhaps who might not be able to persist in their confession to the end, on account of the cruelty of their tormentors, they shall not be found fault with, even though others have been detained on their account. And he brings forward as all instance on this score Gaius and Aristarchus, who were detained instead of Paul; the soldiers who kept Peter; the infants who were massacred by Herod on account of Christ; and Zacharias, the father of the revered and blessed forerunner.

ZONARAS. But if any, says he, have left their possessions, and have gone away, lest being detained they should be endangered, and because, perhaps, they would not be able to persist in their confession unto the end on account of the cruelty of the tormentors, they are not to be accused, even if others are detailed and published on their account. And, again, he brings forward an example from the Acts of the Apostles, saying that at Ephesus also Gaius and Aristarchus were apprehended in the stead of Paul, and that Paul was not blamed for this; nor was Peter, when he was brought forth out of prison by an angel, and escaped the danger, and the soldiers who guarded him were on his account punished. Then he cites another example from the Gospel, namely, the infants who were put to death by Herod; on account of which, says he, our Lord was not blamed. And when Elisabeth had taken to flight with John, and had preserved him, his father Zacharias was put to death, the child being demanded of him; nor was this imputed as a crime to John.

CANON XIV

But if any have endured much violence and the strong pressure of necessity, receiving into their mouths iron and chains, and for their good affection towards the faith have bravely borne the burning of their hands that against their will had been put to the profane sacrifice, as from their prison the thrice-blessed martyrs have written to me respecting those in Libya, and others their fellow-ministers; such, on the testimony of the rest of their brethren, can be placed in the ministry amongst the confessors, as those who have been mortified by many torments, and were no longer able either to speak, or to give utterance, or to move, so as to resist those who vainly offered them violence. For they did not assent to their impiety; as I have again heard from their fellow-ministers, they will be reckoned amongst the confessors, as also he who hath after the example of Timothy ordered his life, obeying him who says, "Follow after righteousness, godliness, faith, love, patience, meekness. Fight the good fight of faith, lay hold on eternal life, whereunto thou art also called, and hast professed a good profession before many witnesses."

BALSAMON. Those who by the violence of the tyrant seemed to eat meat that had been offered to idols, or to drink wine from the Greek libations, – for it happened sometimes that they were thrown upon the ground, and hooks or pieces of iron put into their mouths to keep them open, and then the tyrants poured wine down their throats, or threw into them pieces of meat; or putting hot coals into their hands, together with incense, they compelled them to sacrifice, – if they were clergymen, the canon decrees that they should each in his own degree be ranked amongst the confessors; but if laymen. that they should be reckoned as martyrs, because they did not these things of their own freewill, nor did they at all assent to the action. As also amongst the confessors are to be reckoned those who from the extremity of the tortures lost their strength of body, and were not able to resist those who poured into their mouths the wine of the libations. And next in order he speaks of those who give the testimony of a good conscience, and enumerates them amongst the confessors.

ZONARAS. Those who chastised the blessed martyrs, after many torments, in the case of some violently poured into their mouths the wine of the libations, or even crammed into their mouths some of the meat that had been offered to idols, anti putting incense into their hands, they dragged them to the altars, and then violently seizing on their hands, they either sprinkled the incense upon the altar or placed hot coals together with the incense into their hands, that, not being able to bear the pain of the burning, they might drop the incense together with the coals upon the altar; for they were constrained by them. Men of this sort, he affirms, can remain enrolled in the sacred ministry, or rather be placed in the rank of confessors. For they did not by their own choice either taste the libations, or place the incense upon the altar, but being compelled by violence, their reason not consenting to the action; as also those who from the extremity of the suffering lost their bodily vigour, so as neither to be able to speak or move, nor to resist those who were violently pouring into their months the wine of libations, these also are to be placed amongst the cofessors. And next in order he discourses of those who give the testimony of a good conscience, and places them also in the number of confessors.

CANON XV

No one shall find fault with us for observing the fourth day of the week, and the preparation, on which it is reasonably enjoined us to fast according to the tradition. On the fourth day, indeed, because on it the Jews took counsel for the betrayal of the Lord; and on the sixth, because on it He himself suffered for us. But the Lord's day we celebrate as a day of joy, because on it He rose again, on which day we have received it for a custom not even to bow the knee.

BALSAMON. Conformably to the sixty-fourth Apostolical canon, which decrees that we are not to fast on the Sabbath, with one exception, the great Sabbath; and to the sixty-ninth canon, which severely punishes those who do not fast in the Holy Lent, and on every fourth day of the week and day of preparation. Thus also does the present canon decree.

ZONARAS. Always, says he, are the fourth and sixth days of every week to be kept as fasts; nor will any one find fault with us for fasting on them; and the reasons he subjoins. But on the Lord's day we ought not to fast, for it is a day of joy for the resurrection of the Lord, and on it, says he, we have received that we ought not even to bow the knee. This word, therefore, is to be carefully observed," we have received," and "it is enjoined upon us according to the tradition." For from hence it is evident that long-established custom was taken for law. Moreover, the great Basil annexes also the causes for which it was forbidden to bend the knee on the Lord's day, and from the Passover to Pentecost. Read also the sixty-sixth and sixty-ninth Apostolical canons.

www.ReadHowYouWant.com

You can buy our **Large Type** and **EasyRead** books from our www.ReadHowYouWant.com website, from websites like Amazon.com and through your UK and North American bookshop.

EasyRead books are designed to make your reading easy and enjoyable. **EasyRead** books are published in different font sizes, so you can select the font size best for you.

EasyRead is for people with normal eyesight who want books in an easy-to-read format.

EasyRead Comfort is for people who find reading small print tiring but do not need large print.

EasyRead Large is for people who find it easier to read larger print.

The **EasyRead** font, character, word and line spacing have all been set to make it as easy as possible both to recognize a word, and to run your eye along a line of text without losing your place. We split as few words as possible at line ends, as split words make reading harder and can be annoying. For out-of-copyright books, words have been changed to modern spelling (where the sense is not affected), and the original hyphenation of compound words has been retained where this improves word recognition or sense.

With most things you buy, you get a choice, and you can choose the make and model that suits best. There is a big exception – books. You don't get to choose a format that is easy for you to read – you have to read the format the publisher selects.

This **"One Size Fits All"** paradigm **no longer** need apply to books.

At www.ReadHowYouWant.com, you can order a book just as you want it, so you can read it easily. You can choose nearly any format, and at a surprisingly low cost, because of a technical breakthrough that allows us to typeset an individual book automatically, print and bind the book and have it quickly sent directly to you.

You can have your book in **Talking Book** formats (**DAISY or MP3**) or as an **E-book** or in **Braille**.

We have developed totally new visual formats which we hope will help people with **dyslexia** and other print reading disabilities. Look at www.ReadHowYouWant.com for more information.

Good news for publishers and authors. There is a big market for large type, personalized and accessible format books. We can help publishers and authors find new market opportunities for their books, and selling your book through www.ReadHowYouWant.com is easy – we do the work for you. Contact us on info@ReadHowYouWant.com.

Made in the USA
Monee, IL
08 July 2026

56550364R10046